What are YOU made of?

- Life Lessons From Nature -

Written by Caitlin Nickel
Illustrated by Lilla Vincze

Copyright 2020, author Caitlin Nickel; What are YOU made of? Life lessons from nature.

ISBN: 978-1-7773701-0-7

All rights reserved.

This book or parts thereof may not be reproduced in any form, stored in a retrieval system, or transmitted in any form by any means—'electronic, mechanical, photocopy, recording, or otherwise—without prior written permission of the publisher, except as provided by United States of America copyright law.

Unless otherwise noted, all Scripture quotations are taken from the New King James Version. Copyright 1982 by Thomas Nelson. Used by permission. All rights reserved.

Published by
Caitlin Nickel
Dalmeny, SK
Email: reciprocait@gmail.com

Illustrations by: Lilla Vincze

Interior design by: Giga Studio on Fiverr

Preface

This book was created to showcase how God has lovingly placed examples of His character throughout all of creation.

The four characters highlighted in this book show us what can happen when we trust Him through hard things. My desire is for kids and adults alike to be inspired to meet their present circumstances with bravery.

"...we rejoice in our sufferings, knowing that suffering produces endurance, and endurance produces character, and character produces hope..." (Romans 5:3-5 ESV)

Hi! I'm Pearl. I am famous all over the world and I am sought after for my beauty and elegance. I am one of the most valuable gems on the planet. Look how shiny I am! I am used in all kinds of jewelry from earrings to buttons. I also can come in many different colours. What is your favourite colour? I bet I could be that colour too! I love my beautiful life but it has not always been easy. I started out as something someone else didn't want! I was a pain. A nuisance. An inconvenience. A trial. Do you know how pearls are made? We don't just magically show up in the mouths of oysters. It takes many years, a lot of hard work and much persistence to become what I am now.

There are a couple of different uncomfortable ways that I can be made. Naturally, in the ocean, a shelled

mollusk (like an oyster, snail, clam or mussel) can be invaded by a parasite like a sea worm. These bugs are really hard for the mollusk to spit out and they can be really painful. Ouch! On pearl farms, the farmers very carefully implant a small piece of shell inside the muscle of the mollusk to irritate it. This small piece of shell is also very annoying and really hard to spit out!

After trying and trying to rid itself of the irritant (me) without success, what do you think the mollusk does? Does the mollusk give up and sulk? Does he become very miserable and grumpy? Does he curl up in his bed and wish his life was different? No way! The mollusk was wonderfully designed with the perfect solution to his problem! When the mollusk realizes it cannot get rid of the parasite or the small piece of shell, it begins to coat the irritant in a substance called 'nacre,' which is both lighter AND stronger than concrete! The mollusk continues to produce the nacre and coat the irritant in layer after layer for as long as the mollusk lives, or until the resulting pearl is removed! The longer the irritant is stuck in there, the longer it is coated in nacre and the larger the pearl will be! What a great way to turn a bad situation into something beautiful! If the mollusk was able to just spit out every annoying thing that came its way, I would never have been created! It would have changed history.

As beautiful and famous as I am, I really owe it all to the mollusk who put in all of the time, determination and effort to persevere through a painful situation. I don't know if I was a sea worm that got trapped in the mollusk by accident or if a pearl farmer purposely planted me in there as a piece of shell, but I do know that my mollusk didn't give up!

Fun Fact:

I have been used to create beautiful things since the time of the Ancient Greeks! The whole 16th century in England was known as The Pearl Age because only the very rich or very royal people were allowed to wear pearls.

Grow in PERSEVERANCE!

Complete at least one of these challenges and then write to me to tell me about how it went! When I hear all about your experiment and what you learned I will send you a gift so you can remember how you have grown in perseverance and so you will stay encouraged to keep growing! Refer to copyright page for contact information.

1. Pudding shake

Materials needed:

Blender bottle
Box of pudding mix
Milk

Directions:

Pour the contents of the pudding mix box into the blender bottle along with the amount of milk the box says to use. Pop the blender ball into the bottle and firmly secure the lid onto the bottle. Now… SHAKE!! Don't give up! Keep shaking that bottle! After a few minutes, unscrew the lid and take a peek. What happened? Did you make pudding? Congratulations! Grab a spoon and enjoy. Don't forget to share!

2. Put your art where your mouth is

Materials needed:

    Paint (any type you prefer!)
    Paintbrushes
    Paper
    Painting smock

Directions:

Do you like to paint? Well then this challenge is for YOU! Set up your painting area with paper, paints and brushes. Don't forget to put on a painting smock if you want to keep your clothes clean!

Now, this is where things are going to get wacky! Pick up your paintbrush with your TEETH and paint a picture of Pearl!

Was that fun? I hope you had a lot of laughs. How does your picture look?

Well hello there! I am a pine cone from a Lodgepole Pine tree. My name is Jack!

I may not look as spectacular as Pearl back there but I have a pretty interesting life story too.

For me to fulfill my purpose in life, I sometimes need to be BURNED! With FIRE!

We cones all have inside of us the genetic code of our parent trees. That means we have all the materials we need to make more trees, just like us, already living inside of us. We are FULL of seeds that will hopefully someday be planted into the ground to grow our family. I think we all know how important trees are to the world! Without trees, there would be NO clean air to breathe. Trees and people have a really cool relationship that is called a symbiotic relationship. You humans breathe OUT a gas called carbon

dioxide. If you humans breathe IN carbon dioxide, you would get choked to death because it is really bad for your health! You need clean oxygen to breathe. That's where we trees come in! We breathe in all of that bad carbon dioxide (and all the cow farts) and we breathe OUT clean oxygen. We need each other! That is our main purpose in life. We hold the future right here in our cones. Pretty cool, right?

The only thing is, our cones are sealed inside of us by a hard sticky substance called *resin*. Our seeds are trapped! We will eventually open up on our own, but it can take up to 20 years for that to happen! 20 YEARS! That's where the fire comes in. Wildfires are very destructive. They can ruin many forests and the animals that live in them. BUT! When all seems lost, beneath ashy soil new hope is sprouting. That fire has melted away the resin that keeps our seeds sealed up. It actually has helped us! That fire may have been hot (it was) and it may have been terrifying (it REALLY was!) but because of it, new life has taken root.

Fun Fact:

The Lodgepole Pinecone is not the only one that does well after a fire has unsettled it! Some Eucalyptus trees have new buds hidden under their bark and if a fire harms the bark, it reveals the new buds and they begin to grow!

Grow in HOPE!

Complete at least one of these challenges and then write to me to tell me about how it went! When I hear all about your experiment and what you learned I will send you a gift so you can remember how you have grown in hope and so you will stay encouraged to keep growing! Refer to copyright page for contact information.

1. Make a family goal list

Materials needed:

Markers
A jar
Construction paper
Scissors

Directions:

Cut the construction paper into 1 inch thick strips.

Sit down as an entire family and come up with as many ideas you can think of for goals you all want to meet over the next 12 months.

Do you want to have less screen time? Do you want to go on more walks together? Do you want to read together more?

Whenever someone comes up with an idea, write it on a strip of paper and stick it in the jar!

Over the next 12 months take turns picking a paper out of the jar and work on it together as a family!

2. Three stars and a wish

Materials needed:

A piece of paper
Markers
Stickers

Directions:

Sit down in a quiet place with your markers, your stickers and your paper. Draw three large stars down the left side of the paper. Colour them however you want! Beside each star write down something you are REALLY good at! Can you draw really well? Can you make people laugh?

Under the last star on the page draw a large cloud. Beside the cloud write down one thing you could get better at. Would you like to be more kind to your brother or sister? Do you want to win a race?

After writing out your three stars and your wish, decorate the page however you want. On the backside of the page, list some ways you can make your wish come true!

I know you recognize me! I'm Diamond! It is so great to meet you.

I see you met my friend Pearl earlier. Isn't she great? She and I have a lot in common. We are both valuable gems, we are both a symbol of status and we are both super shiny! Check out all of this sparkle! I'm not just beautiful and valuable though. I'm also SUPER strong! Do you think you can break me with a hammer? Nope! The only thing that can leave even a scratch on me is another diamond. I am so precious and useful that people often risk their lives to find me! Another thing that Pearl and I have in common is the fact that we both began life under some pretty tough circumstances...

Where do YOU think diamonds come from? We certainly don't grow on trees! That would be easy. Well let me tell you how it really happens...

Under your feet right now, 100 miles beneath the Earth's surface is a place called the mantle. This layer deep inside our planet separates the ground you walk on from the molten lava layer beneath it.

Do you like to do puzzles? Think of your favourite puzzle. If you put that puzzle together on a hard flat surface, the pieces stay put where they are supposed to. If you were to lay that puzzle in a puddle of water, the pieces would float away from each other. They may even smash into each other or overlap! Our Earth's surface is a little like that. It is made out of puzzle-like pieces called tectonic plates. When two of these plates overlap, all of the natural materials on the surface of the bottom plate (like snail shells and grass) get trapped inside the mantle layer. Do you have ANY IDEA how HOT it is down there? Imagine the hottest summer day you can think of. Got it? Ok now, think even HOTTER! The oven in your house gets as hot as 500 degrees Celsius. The mantle can range from 1000 degrees Celsius to 3700 degrees Celsius!! Can you even imagine that kind of heat? I wouldn't be able to unless I had seen it for myself. And I did. Not only was it unthinkably hot and uncomfortable down there but I was also under an ENORMOUS amount of pressure! How much pressure? Well, it would be like having 1400 elephants standing on your head! YIKES!

There I was, being helplessly blazed upon by the staggering heat and being crushed by the intense pressure. Did I want to escape? Yes. Did I want it to be over? Yes! Did I feel like I couldn't take even one more second of it?! YES!! But you know what? It was at that point that something amazing happened. I held on tight and before I knew it I wasn't just a piece of decaying snail. I was a DIAMOND. You want to know what else? I would do it all again. Under just the right heat and just the right pressure for just the right amount of time, I was transformed into something AMAZING. If I had quit and somehow escaped before that transformative moment came, I would have never known how truly strong and beautiful I could be.

Fun Fact:

Small bits of me are sometimes placed in oil drilling equipment to make the drills more powerful to cut through hard materials. I'm even used in some computers! I am so versatile

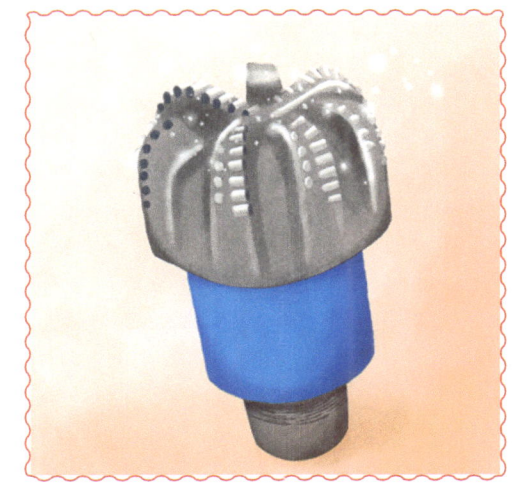

Grow in STRENGTH!

Complete at least one of these challenges and then write to me to tell me about how it went! When I hear all about your experiment and what you learned I will send you a gift so you can remember how you have grown in strength and so you will stay encouraged to keep growing! Refer to copyright page for contact information.

1. Crab walk

Materials needed:

Your amazing body
A floor
A friend

Directions:

Find a clear space on the ground or the floor and lay down on your back. Now bend your knees and plant your feet firmly on the ground. Bend your elbows and plant your open hands (palm down) firmly on the ground. Using your elbows, hands and feet, lift your body off the ground until only your feet and your hands are holding you up. Now, crawl like a crab!

Crabs walk sideways but you can walk forwards, backwards, sideways, however! For added fun, ask a friend or a family member to crab race you!

2. Soup can flyers

Materials needed:

Two large soup cans

Directions:

Take the two large soup cans, one in each hand. Stand straight with your arms at your sides. Now, take a deep breath and lift the cans up until they are parallel to your shoulders. In a controlled manner, bring your arms back down to your sides. Repeat 15 times. Take a 3-minute break. Do another 15 Soup Can Flyers.

You can make this harder or easier by increasing or decreasing the repetitions.

Did you feel your muscles getting stronger?

Good day to you.

Go ahead and just GUESS what I am. Go ahead.

What's that? I look like sea coral? Well I take that as a compliment! But I am not a type of sea coral.

Pardon me? I also look like a piece of chewed up bubblegum that's been dropped on the sand?!? Well... I guess I sort of do. I promise though, I am something MUCH more incredible! Are you ready for this??

My name is Fulgurite. Say it with me. "Fool-geh-right." You almost have it, try again: Fulgu...oh never mind. It's a mouthful even for me. My friends call me Fergie anyway, so you might as well call me that too.

I may not look like anything special but I really am special and I'm

very, very rare.

If you were to pick me up, you would be holding LIGHTNING!

You're probably thinking "Stop right there, Fergie. You have lost your chewing-gum mind. I know what lightning is and..."

But wait! Hear me out.

When there is a big powerful

storm and lightning strikes clean sand or a rocky mountain top, the intense heat actually MELTS the sand or rock particles together and forms... ME. Fulgurite. A very rare type of glass. Once lightning strikes the sand and melts it into me, then I stay in the exact same shape of the lightning when it struck! I'm sort of like fossilized lightning. Isn't that amazing? Did I mention that I'm very rare?

Lightning is very powerful and very dangerous. BUT as you can see: lightning can also be very creative!

I started out as a patch of regular sand and then BOOM! I am lightning you can hold. In an instant, something completely unexpected, and to be honest quite painful, happened to me and I was transfigured into something rare and wonderful. Don't get me wrong! I was very happy being sand. I had no complaints! I could have been sand forever. I never in a million years would have ASKED to be struck by lightning. But I was. And not only did I survive but... look at me now! I am a moment of incredible power frozen in time forever.

Fun Fact:

I can be very fragile! When a very large piece of me is found, I am often removed from where I am found in smaller pieces and then glued back together later.

Grow in POWER!

Complete at least one of these challenges and then write to me to tell me about how it went! When I hear all about your experiment and what you learned I will send you a gift so you can remember how you have grown in power and so you will stay encouraged to keep growing! Refer to copyright page for contact information.

1. "Magically" separate salt and pepper

Materials needed:

- A comb
- A small dish
- Salt
- Pepper
- A person with hair

Directions:

Pour ½ cup of salt and 1/8 cup of pepper into a small dish. Stir! Now take the comb and give it a static charge by running it through your hair*. Take that charged up comb and hold it over the dish. What happened?? Did the pepper magically jump up onto the comb?

*The person who charges the comb is the person who has to also hold the comb abover the salt and pepper dish. If a person charges the comb and then hands it off to another person, it will lose its charge. You can try this as a bonus experiment as well!

2. Potato battery

Materials needed:

Two large russet potatoes
2 zinc nails
Knife
Small LED lightbulb

6 alligator clips
Two 2" pieces of thick copper wire
Three 4" pieces of thin copper wire

Adult supervision/assistance required

Directions:

Make two 1" slits on each end of each potato with a knife (make sure to ask an adult for help with this!).

Now put one piece of the thick copper wire in the slit in one end of each potato and a nail in the slit in the other end of each potato.

Next, take the three pieces of thin copper wire and connect the alligator clips onto each end of those strips by wrapping the wire around the back of the clip (not the alligator mouth part).

Connect one of alligator clips from one of the thin pieces of wire onto the thicker copper wire in the end of the first potato, and then attach the other side of the clip onto the base of the lightbulb.

Take a second piece of thin wire and attach one of its alligator clips onto the base of the lightbulb as well. Take the clip on other end of that same wire and clip it onto the nail on the second potato.

Now (ALMOST done!) take the last piece of thin wire and attach one end to the thicker wire in the end of the second potato. Attach the clip on the other end of that same wire onto the nail in the first potato.

What happens to the lightbulb?? Did it light up? If it did, why did that happen? Do some research with your parents to find out!

Final Thoughts...

Can you think of something hard you have had to face? What sort of beautiful thing could be made of your situation if you don't give up?

God has lovingly created all of these wonderful reminders in nature that when we choose to live our lives for Him, we can do hard things! When we meet any kind of challenge (and life will be full of challenges), we can ask for God's help and guidance. He will be faithful and use even the most difficult of challenges to grow us. To change us. To make us more like Him.

We will develop perseverance like a Pearl...

Our lives will become something beautiful, useful and strong like the Diamond...

He will use us to plant new life and hope for the future like the Pinecones...

We will point to the awesome power of who He is and what He can do like the Fulgurite...

What other reminders of God's great love and design can you find in nature?

www.ingramcontent.com/pod-product-compliance
Lightning Source LLC
Chambersburg PA
CBHW042257100526
44589CB00003B/59